EARTHWORKS
SELECTED POEMS

EARTHWORKS
SELECTED POEMS

ROSANNA WARREN

American Philosophical Society Press
Philadelphia • 2016

Transactions of the

American Philosophical Society
Held at Philadelphia
For Promoting Useful Knowledge
Volume 106, Part 1

ISBN: 978-1-60618-061-7
U.S. ISSN: 0065-9746

Library of Congress Cataloging-in-Publication Data

Names: Warren, Rosanna, author.
Title: Earthworks : selected poems / Rosanna Warren.
Description: Philadelphia, PA : American Philosophical Society Press, 2016.
Identifiers: LCCN 2016021081 | ISBN 9781606180617 (alk. paper)
Classification: LCC PS3573.A7793 A6 2016 | DDC 811/.54—dc23
LC record available at https://lccn.loc.gov/2016021081

CONTENTS

From *Departure* (2003)

From *Ghost in a Red Hat* (2011)

INTRODUCTION

I have arranged the poems in this volume chronologically, from early to more recent in my first four collections of poetry. I place them under the protection of two poetry saints: William Blake and Hart Crane. The Blake of "London" inspires my work and my life, in the calling to wander about, to be marginal, from the margins to observe, to insist that justice matters:

> I wander thro' each charter'd street.
> Near where the charter'd Thames does flow
> And mark in every face I meet
> Marks of weakness, marks of woe.

For Blake, there is no such thing as a private life or a private love immune from the larger systems in which we struggle. I agree. I hope my poems agree.

They take another direction from Hart Crane. Not justice, but sacrifice: a conviction that we shall not be spared being broken, and that out of brokenness will arise a truthful music and gifts of honesty and love: "And so it was I entered the broken world/ To trace the visionary company of love . . . " ("The Broken Tower").

Blake's chartered streets, Crane's broken world, appear in many forms in my poems, and form is the key: It is the task of the poem to make new form from fractured language, fractured experience. At times I focus on the historical and the national, as in "After," a poem about Hurricane Katrina, and the long poem dedicated to Frederick Law Olmsted, "Earthworks." In "After," I mourn for my country, which I have seen destroying itself these last two decades:

> A highway straight to the end of the world skims past
> a ruined mall . . .

In "Earthworks," I summon the ghost of Olmsted to remind us what it is to design a democratic space out of mud and muck, and to preserve that space. But the vision of love and justice extends beyond national boundaries: "From the Notebooks of Anne Verveine" meditates on an essential and metaphysical homelessness, the state that underlies our illusions of safety. The poems of private eros, maternal love, illness, and mourning explore our vulnerability as we come to know it most intimately. Poems have work to do: to bear witness, to cry out, to lament, to praise. They should be psalms for their time.

Rosanna Warren

Rosanna Warren is the Hanna Holborn Gray Distinguished Service Professor in the Committee on Social Thought at the University of Chicago. Her book of criticism, *Fables of the Self: Studies in Lyric Poetry,* came out in 2008. Her most recent books of poems are *Departure* (2003) and *Ghost in a Red Hat* (2011). She is the recipient of awards from the Academy of American Poets, The American Academy of Arts and Letters, the Lila Wallace Foundation, the Guggenheim Foundation, and the New England Poetry Club, among others. She was a Chancellor of the Academy of American Poets from 1999 to 2005, and is a member of the American Academy Arts and Letters, the American Academy of Arts and Sciences, and the American Philosophical Society.

Funerary Portraits

In a world of stone, they grieve in stone.

1 / *Mother*

The mother presses her head to her hand, already
bowing under the weight
of her strange childlessness, while the child
like the child still uncarved somewhere, reaches out
to the figure who sits, half-veiled,
dazed, with a small box on her lap
containing those objects—comb,
perfume vial, jade necklace—which she will take
with her to a world where they can no longer be used
and where beauty is not an issue.

2 / Hunter

His dogs would follow him. They are pure
energy pent in arabesques of tails,
curling spines, arched necks. But they are held
back by the small servant who knows
his master, this time, has no quarry.
In marble, they whine, and scratch. But he, the young
huntsman whose ordinary brow has
cleared suddenly and widened into something
like an ideal proportion, has no ear
for them. He listens, instead, to a new
chorus of voices, not animal, not
human, but as though
eucalyptus leaves sharpened each
other, blade scraping on blade, and
for the fulfillment of the ceremony, waited,
only for him.

3 / *Timarista* and *Krito*

Her fingers on the girl's bare neck, light
and possessive, the girl's head lowered,
arm raised, chiton spilling like water
across uptilting breasts—if these two
are mother and daughter, how
erotic to have given birth, how
the young one—the live one—folds still further
toward the embrace, her silk in flight
from tiny clasps, while Timarista, the elder, stands
column-fluted, staring beyond
the whorls of Krito's
hair, ear, drapery, her past
pleasure knotted in this girl and now
released, so that she half-
turns, her free left arm
thrust out, away, hand open as though
to seize on a new life.

Alps

The mountains taught us speechlessness.
A snowshoe hare loped to its place

in silence, through powder. We spoke
only below, in the village, and then
of merely human absences, as when
G. departed, taken sick,

or when we had to conclude affairs
that had not been love, or even,
often, affairs—conclude them in
haste, with our hats on, there by the stairs:

for whatever they'd been, they had
at least composed the bleak-
ness. And hard enough it had been to speak
of those un-mountainous matters, in few words, without fraud.

History as Decoration

Float over us, Florence, your banners
of assassination, your most expensive
reds: Brazil, Majorca lichen, cochineal.
Let the Neoplatonic Arno flow
crocus yellow. Let palazzo walls,
flaunt quattrocento dyes: "little
monk" and "lion skin." We pay for beauty; beautiful
are gorgeous crimes we cannot feel—

they shone so long ago. And those philosophies
too pretty in spirit ever to be real.
City of fashion. Leonardo chose
the hanged Pazzi conspirator for a theme:
"Tawny cap; black satin vest," he wrote,
"black sleeveleas coat, lined; turquoise
jacket lined with fox; Bernardo di
Bandino Baroncigli; black hose."

So dangled the elegant corpse, *bella figura*
though its tongue stuck out. The keen, gossipy
faces still peer from Ghirlandaio's walls
and from the streets we elbow through today.
History flashes in banknotes. Gold, jade, corals
twinkle from hand to hand, while the spectral glare
of Savonarola's sunset bonfire licks the square
and his cries ascend and blend with Vespers bells.

To Max Jacob

You were a moral dandy, sir. The font
could have twinkled with eau-de-cologne
for all you cared; the point
was only the soul's toilette, to keep
malicious Max immaculate. The stone
on which you knelt was bare,
the walls you prayed to innocent
of any devil's ornament. And yet
your piety is touching, though
(because?) histrionic: grown
old with the actor, the gesture must
approach perfection of artifice.
Superbly you litter your skull with dust,
raise up trembling lips to kiss
the godly Host. You've scarce a hair
but yank what you can, by God,
right out at the roots.
A fourteen-year scenario
of Job on ash-heap, vile,
repentant, all the while
so deadly bored you write your friends,
"The quality of work depends
all, on the *kind* of boredom."
What interior desert did you fear
so terribly, you chose
a monk's cell, not the city, for your stage?
And for your major prop, the rose
of Christ, and not of Baudelaire?

Max Jacob at Saint Benoît

The noonday square. Plane leaves, dust:
they scurry in heat shimmering gusts.
Even shadows rustle. The Belgians are gone.
The tiny terrier trots alone.
Max prayed here, *le grand poseur,*
salon mystic and *littérateur,*
but fourteen years, remember, that's one hell
of a pose for a Paris swell.
He had an infallible sense of scene.
See that stone soul torn limb from limb
between the devils and seraphim?
Romanesque, of course, for Max to preen
his own soul's pretty plumage here
year after tiresome dusty year.
And still, it wasn't easy. *Quel ennui!*
This flat, hot land, the sluggish Loire;
daily, nightly, daily: *prière, devoir;*
no more blue-yellow visions of Christ on the tree
(from Max's aquarelle), no more *cinémathèque*
blue movie Maries scolding *"pauvre Max"*
(to scandalize confessors),
no more dandified mystics dogging his tracks.
At Saint Benoît, just dust. The trek
to God? Beyond the crypt, it led
from boredom to boredom to prison camp bed
in Drancy. There, the Nazis let him die
—an old Jew with pneumonia—"naturally."

Renoir

for Donald Davie

Under striped flutter of awnings, they have come
together this afternoon to glitter with
carafes and wine glasses, and the fluffy dog
perched on the table amid parings
of apples and peaches. They rehearse
a civilization here among
bright collaborations of sun. The two
gentlemen nearest us take their ease
bare-armed, in undershirts. At the next
table, brown jacket and bowler melt
into ingenious dapple and nonchalance,
and only the farthest gentlemen, vertical, sustain
in suits and top hats, a dark
decorum. And ladies, ladies—
bonneted, buttoned at neck
and wrists, yet ripe
with sleep: their cheeks
and half-closed eyes give them away.
Flesh is fruit, whispers brush and sunlight
wine; all cloth
dissolves. And when these chroma
and characters have faded
into the single, sensual blur of an afternoon
lost, there will remain
ghostly vermilion, hieroglyphic lips,
awning stripes and anemones that once
so vulgarly blazed, now dimming to
the mystic map of sprawl, spatter, and glare:
not Jeanne, Marie-Thérèse, Alphonse, Auguste, but this—
this truest pattern, radiance revealed,
a constellation visible at dusk.

"Ille mi par . . . "

(Catullus LI, from Sappho)

He's like a god, that man; he seems
(if this can be) to shine beyond
the gods, who nestling near you sees
 you and hears you

laughing low in your throat. It tears me
apart. For when I glimpse you,
Lesbia, look—I'm helpless:
 tongue a frozen

lump, and palest fire
pouring through all my limbs; my ears
deafened in ringing; each eye
 shuttered in night.

. . . . .

You're wasting your time, Catullus,
laying waste to your life. You love it;
Whole kingdoms and blissful cities
 have wasted away, like you.

Catullus XI

Furius and Aurelius, you fine friends
of Catullus, whether he forces his way
to farthest India where the Eastern shore
    unrolls, booming in surf;

whether he trudges among Hyrcanians, languid
Arabs, Scythians, Parthian bowmen, or
along that delta stained by the seven
    mouths of the Nile;

whether he marches clear over the Alps and there
surveys great Caesar's dominions,
the Gallic Rhine, and savage, far-off, un-
    imaginable Britons—

you who would traipse with your dear friend all
over the world, wherever the gods' design
might call, just take to my darling
    this little message:

let her live, let her flourish, with all her lovers,
let her seize in her cunt three hundred at a time
loving none, but time and again exploding
    their bloated members.

But she'd better not look, like last time, for my
love reviving. It's her fault it's fallen
a flower at the rim of the meadow, touched
    by the plow passing.

Season Due

They are unforgiving and do not ask mercy, these last
of the season's flowers: chrysanthemums, brash
marigolds, fat sultan dahlias a-nod

    in rain. It is
    September. Pansy
    freaked with jet be

damned: it takes this radiant bitterness to
stand, to take the throb of sky, now sky
is cold, falls bodily, assaults. In tangled

    conclave, spiky-
    leaved, they
    wait. The news

is fatal. Leaf by leaf, petal
by petal, they brazen out this chill
which has felled already gentler flowers and herbs

    and now probes
    these veins for a last
    mortal volley of

cadmium orange, magenta, a last acrid flood
of perfume that will drift in the air here once more,
yet once more, when these stubborn flowers have died.

Hagar

And the water was spent in the bottle, and she cast the child under one of the
shrubs. (Gen. 21:15)

Was it a mountain wavering on the rim
of sky, or only air, shaken like a flame?
Dust stung my nostrils. Lizards fled
over the sharp track where my feet had bled.
My sandal thongs were broken. The water was gone.
I cracked the jar, it cracked like an old bone.
Lord of the desert, did you bless
that birth? Bonded to Abraham, did I guess
his wilderness? He thrust
us out from the squandering of his lust
after I'd framed its future. Hers as well,
griping mistress whose belly would not swell,
witch whose hair I brushed and wound in braids,
whose robe I stitched, whose veil I decked with beads
to snag his pleasure. What was left my own?
Not my bought body, surely. Not my son.
Only that core of shock from which he surged,
the spasm that unbonded me, and purged
me of Master and Mistress and the Lord.
I pressed my knees to the rock, and poured
my body out like sand across the sand.
Not to see him die, I pressed my hand
into my sockets, but his cry broke through
all bone and fiber, shattered the sealed blue
of heaven to wound your vast and hovering ear,
Lord of the desert, Lord who cannot hear
our prayers, but the deathwail of a child
startling from the rootclutch in the wild.

You are the God of stone and stony eyes
and water dripping through stone crevices
to the swollen tongue that cannot taste your name.
Lord of thistle and mica. Here I am.

Le Ventre de Paris:
A Marriage Poem

I
La Rue Montorgeuil: the Market

They built the church here, imagining
He would come
to these cobbles, these streaming gutters,
the white pig's head skinned with drowsing eyes;
He would finger
dahlia petals mashed in the sewer,
chicken clutch, eel coil, choirs
of shrimp;
He would touch you, touch
me, because we are equally
soiled, because butchery
is life, and life runs
in us as down this street.

II
St. Eustache: the Market Church

The little we know
of St. Eustache
becomes him: how
this Roman (third
century A.D.) general

while hunting beheld
a crucifix
in a stag's antlers
and instantly
converted; how

broiled
in an iron bull, his cries
converted
to music; how, trans-
lated, he blesses

this butchers' cathedral,
its stained glass, its *clochards,*
its organ recitals,
its street
whistling with market blood.

Child Model

for Rosalie Carlson

(Greenland Eskimo mummy, boy, four years old,
National Geographic, February 1985)

I want to adopt you, doll-like child,
your death, your *National*
Geographic resurrection. Cold

has clasped you in its cache, all
gaze, all glimmer. Arctic star,
cuddled in sealskin grave-creche, still

you wait there for your mother,
trusting she'll trudge back through the snow,
famine, centuries: lift you from this glamour,

snatch you, full-limbed, laughing home. But now
in these pages, trapped, you touch
for comfort tiny beads of bone. We know

nothing of you save that such
patient beauty, still unputrefied,
was never seen in death. We clutch

you, ancient child: we need
to think you're saved, as if one face unmarred
in Kodachrome rescued all others who have died

ugly, bruised, disqualified.

Science Lessons

The human body is superfluous.
Rochester knew it: lurching home
from a night of swiving and sluicing,
ballocks crumpled, loins wrung out,
fingers dripping and pungent, he was consumed

by knowledge. Having caressed
the soft slippage of flesh from rib and hip,
foreknew rack, gibbet, kettle, all the precise
instruments of quest including
the final, eloquent shudder; knew

pond scum to grow gooseflesh, to be
as freakishly aroused; knew Spanish moss
to dangle as lace, black mud to suck
and ooze with a confession of pleasure;
knew truth a prisoner

begging to be shucked free.
So over and over the glossy girl,
the sleek-limbed boy, must pose
while Love the scientist stutters, repeats himself
staggers through his garbled litanies

husking pure form from the body of this death.

The Cost

That wasn't our baby
in the trashcan in the city zoo
someone else picked it out someone
else wrapped it in paper and dropped it in

    Why do you sleep
    with your back to me

Besides it's another city we don't
live there anymore

    Because it's cold

Besides I collect
phrases these days not babies
Spartan   clasp   jute finish   crotch island

    Last winter was colder
    we lived by the Swedenborgian Institute
    where you had your accident

Or that list of words from the summer in Florence
the essential list warm clues
like *sausage   torture   bilge* I knew
I'd need the rest of my life

but I lost it

    The ice at the corner scared me

My hands soiled with news

That wasn't our baby

Virginity   elocution   electrocution
light sliding off the ailanthus spikes

It was another city

It was still breathing

The cost of empire is great and disturbing
the secret knowledge of philosophy

We weren't the ones

Ice

Lawn a mastodon's matted hide
Roof shingles dinosaur skin

From the fencepost a crow
watches afternoon throttle the small white house

Clouds unskeining from the maple's hands

Down from his front porch
he steps
        the old
man

pauses

Tests
        his balance

on a slab of light

In Creve Coeur, Missouri

(Pulitzer Prize for photojournalism, 1989)

Only in Creve Coeur
would an amateur photographer
firebug snap a shot so
unconsolable: fireman bent low

over the rag of body held
like impossible laundry pulled
too soon from the line, too pale,
too sodden with smoke to flail

in his huge, dark, crumpled embrace.
He leans to the tiny face.
Her hair stands out like flame.
She is naked, she has no name.

No longer a baby, almost
a child, not yet a ghost,
she presses a doll-like fist
to his professional chest.

Her head falls back to his hand.
Tell us that she will stand
again, quarrel and misbehave.
He is trying to make her breathe.

Strong man, you know how it's done,
you've done it again and again
sucking the spirit back
to us for its lair of smoke.

We'll call it a fine surprise.
The snapshot won a prize
though it couldn't revive *her*
that night in Creve Coeur.

The Cormorant

for Eunice

Up through the buttercup meadow the children lead
their father. Behind them, gloom
of spruce and fir, thicket through which they pried
into the golden ruckus of the field, toward home:

this rented house where I wait for their return
and believe the scene eternal. They have been out
studying the economy of the sea. They trudged to earn
sand dollars, crab claws, whelk shells, the huge debt

repaid in smithereens along the shore:
ocean, old blowhard, wheezing in the give
and take, gulls grieving the shattered store.
It is your death I can't believe,

last night, inland, away from us, beyond
these drawling compensations of the moon.
If there's an exchange for you, some kind of bond,
it's past negotiation. You died alone.

Across my desk wash memories of ways
I've tried to hold you: that poem of years ago
starring you in your *mater dolorosa* phase;
or my Sunday picnic sketch in which the show

is stolen by your poised, patrician foot
above whose nakedness the party floats.
No one can hold you now. The point is moot.
I see you standing, marshaling your boats

23

of gravy, chutney, cranberry, at your vast
harboring Thanksgiving table, fork held aloft
while you survey the victualing of your coast.
We children surged around you, and you laughed.

Downstairs, the screen door slams, and slams me back
into the present, which you do not share.
Our children tumble in, they shake the pack
of sea-treasures out on table, floor, and chair.

But now we tune our clamor to your quiet.
The deacon spruces keep the darkest note
though hawkweed tease us with its saffron riot.
There are some wrecks from which no loose planks float,

nothing the sea gives back. I walked alone
on the beach this morning, watching a cormorant
skid, thudding, into water. It dove down
into that shuddering darkness where we can't

breathe. Impossibly long. Nothing to see.
Nothing but troughs and swells
over and over hollowing out the sea.
And, beyond the cove, the channel bells.

Necrophiliac

More marrow to suck, more elegies
to whistle through the digestive track. So help
me God to another dollop of death,
come on strong with the gravy and black-eyed peas,
slop it all in the transcendental stew
whose vapors rise and shine in the nostrils of heaven.
Distill the belches, preserve the drool as ink:
Death, since you nourish me, I'll flatter you
inordinately. Consumers both, with claws
cocked and molars prompt at the fresh-dug grave,
reaper and elegist, we collaborate
and batten in this strictest of intimacies,
my throat an open sepulchre, my tongue
forever groping grief forever young.

Song

    A yellow coverlet
    in the greenwood:
spread the corners wide to the dim, stoop-shouldered pines.
    Let blank sky
    be your canopy.
Fringe the bedspread with the wall of lapsing stones.
    Here faith has cut
    in upright granite
"Meet me in Heaven" at the grave of each child
    lost the same year,
    three, buried here,
a century ago. Roots and mosses hold
    in the same bed
    mother, daughter, dead
together, in one day. "Lord, remember the poor,"
    their crumbling letters pray.
    I turn away.
I shall meet you nowhere, in no transfigured hour.
    On soft, matted soil
    blueberry bushes crawl,
each separate berry a small, hot globe of tinctured sun.
    Crushed on the tongue
    it releases a pang
of flesh. Tender flesh, slipped from its skin,
    preserves its blue heat
    down my throat.

The Broken Pot

for ECW

The Mother is present in every house. Need I break the news as one breaks an earthen pot on the floor? Rampräsäd (1718–1775)

I

I am far from you, I am walking farther
down the peninsular road in a borrowed landscape.
From the soggy meadow, a red cow and her calf
observe me, and go on munching. They are densely matted
with rain. They stand their ground. Raindrops bedeck
the rusty tractor parked at the edge of the field,
the barbed wire, the arcing boughs of wintergreen
weighted down with garnet berries.
At the far rim of the field, skeletal oaks
and birches stalk the shore of a tidal inlet
and I stride on, through drizzle, down the road
to the summer cottages in their winter autism,
to the last spine of rock dragged bare by the tide.
There, at the farthest verge, the open sea
is merely an intuition through shawled mist.

The road loops back. Evening closes in,
I let the road have its way and lead me home.
By now, the cow and her calf must be in the barn.
Their meadow lies open in the seeping light.
I am absentminded. But the cattle,
standing quietly together, had shaped the field,
and shape it still in their absence, breathing
together in the ruminant, gaseous dark
where I cannot see them.

27

II
Your Christmas narcissi, too leggy for their frills,
pitched from your table.
You had thought the bulbs were onions, kept them
refrigerated in the vegetable drawer
and narrowly missed a very bitter stew.
You are alone in your rooms
where the Braque bird spreads broad wings
over your past, sheltering in his flight
so many losses
              that your thinness now
seems the very principle of subtraction
as if light were carving you away before our eyes.

III
And Rome rises
in your mind, ruinous and fecund
as in your girlhood when you foresaw,
looking back,

in its columns, arches, esplanades,
processions, prisoners, imperial gore
the fountain jet
of all our human life, that glittering arc:

foresaw
plazzas, domes, receding colonnades
scooped out of solitude

the internal city
a habitable beauty
subsisting on disappearance

monument to which I turn now
with my tribute
of broken shards, my *symbolon*

from the original vessel in whose clay we share.

Hellenistic Head

for Derek Walcott

She's in two worlds, her veil blown half across her face:
hair a dense crown of hyacinth knots, her one
visible eye gone blank. How to make marble drift
like muslin, like sea mist, across a brow?
Under the scarf, the daydream stirs:

                               gash in the morning torn
by the white horse loosed, careening
across two parkway lanes and up the median grass,
thunder made flesh in haunches and arcing neck
as cars streamed by like a doubled Milky Way
and two small dark figures, arms upraised,
jostled along the highway shoulder, swinging rope.
We were children, nestled by speed into the backseat
of our speeding car. The horse was a comet,
mane and tail igniting a drizzled day.

And we are gone in the hurtling car, my brother and I,
forty years gone in that torrent of fumes and chrome
that snatched away childhood house and barn and the
                               hummocky field,
slow-syrup hours of Sunday afternoons
with creaky floorboards and spiders curled in the knotholes of
                               beams,
and the demigods who drove the car and admonished us
and conversed unknowably in the sanctum of the front seat.

The horse's eyes bulged yogurt-white from bloody rims,
big as croquet balls and veiny with panic,
but sparked, too, with glee
to see his world so streamingly wide and fast.
He was likely, it was clear, to be horribly hurt.
He was likely to kill people.
                                    In the Hellenistic head,
half the face freezes in the fully empty gaze.
The other half is stone that turns into wind.

Arrival

(Poseidon, *Iliad* XIII)

That's how a god descends from a mountain peak
in Samothrace: startled attention stirs him, then
three strides vault him down to the plain as oak roots shake
and boulders lurch from the cliff face, vomiting down

its loosened jaw of scree: that's how a god descends,
the fourth stride thunders him into his harbor pool
at Aigai where, gold in the weedy depths, his palace bends
the sun beams: golden the armor he buckles, all

sun-hammered glint and gleam the bridles he fastens
on golden-maned horses, his whip a gold parabola in foam,
chariot a churning glare on a wave that glistens:
that's how a god arrives, how grief will come

any day, any ordinary hour, when all we see
is a peculiar, shivering brilliance in the air
like a premonition of migraine; and no one can see
later, how in such a flash, the dark came there.

"Departure"

(from Max Beckmann and Guido Guinizelli)

"I can only speak to people who—"

Unspeaking, unspoken, the full-breasted woman
tied to a dead man upside down

stands center stage with a lamp in her hand,
sheds kerosene glow on the marching band.

That's Cupid, the dark dwarf who tightens her rope:
this is art, this is love, that's the classical shape

of proscenium arch. This is Germany, May '32,
" . . . can only speak to people who

already carry, consciously or unconsciously, within them—"

You want to buy that center panel, Lilly, but
You can't have that alone

There will always be, on one side, a man bound to a column
with both hands chopped off; there will always be
a still life with hand grenade grapes and a woman kneeling
before an executioner who swings a bag of iron fish

Love always shelters in the gentle heart

And you will always—won't you?—find yourself groping
in a dark stairwell ill-lit by the feeble, dangerous lamp
while you drag along, strapped to you, the corpse of all your
                                        errors,
and the drum throbs and shudders like a titanic heart

33

Love's fire is kindled in the gentle heart
as light kindles in a precious gem

And there's another romance, in which the woman
And man are strapped to each other alive, but head to feet,
                                        on a giant fish
and each holds in hand the ritual mask of the other
as they hurtle downward toward a brilliant engulfing ocean

        as the star beam strikes the water
        but the sky keeps the star and all its fire

which is generally known as love. No, you can't
buy the central panel alone, with the king and queen
joyous and powerful in their open boat, the baby bespeaking
                                        freedom
and the net full of fish flashing in blessed abundance

"—who already, carry consciously or unconsciously, within them
a similar metaphysical code."

        because the oarsman is blindfolded
        because the crowned fisherman has his back to us
        because that open boat
        has not set sail
        from our shores,
        nor will it, while we are alive.

Mud

for John Walker

It's not as simple as rhyming "mud" and "blood"
    as Owen did and does ("I, too, saw God through mud")
    in his "Apologia."
Or feces and "fecit" which is
    a kind of rhyme as in
    "Walker fecit," which he

did and does through,
    mud, bruised flesh, pigment, glossy
    oil pressed from memory's trench:
"God" rhymes of course with
    everything. It's not enough
    to spread damp clay ("Was it for this

the clay grew tall?") across canvas: he can't
    bury fathers, uncles,
    sons, they keep
sprouting, worms their words ("Men went
    to Catraeth as day
    dawned"): Our words, his

words: Aneirin, Jones, a seethe on
    the surface we cannot
    possess. The dead belong
to no one, live their own
    maggoty life observed
    by the small, sheep-skulled soldier;

by the father who clambers out of the painter's skull;
      by the easel which wants
      to be lantern and cross.
The Somme? July 1, 1916: men went, men
      want: all those men marched
      which century? Sixth? The

Welsh at Catraeth, three hundred dead: a sum:
      a song. Whose ribcage
      gapes? Whose numbers ooze
in the ditch of years? This painter comes
      too late. He hoists
      his loop of pods upon

a firmament of mud, he hangs dark swags
      of script and
      sacrament. (A
duchess approves. She likes chiaro-
      scuro in love and
      war). The painter has brought

a necklace—no, a rosary— of human
      kidneys, slick
      and soiled. It is
not as easy as rhyming "mud"
      and "blood." The words belong
      to no one. (Not that we

wanted. Not that we wanted to know.)

Island in the Charles

"By being scholar first of that new night"
(Crashaw)

Taking the well-worn path in the mind though dusk encroaches
upon the mind, taking back alleys careful step by step
past parked cars and trash containers, three blocks to the
                                                    concrete ramp
of the footbridge spanning the highway with its rivering
                                                    four-lane
unstaunchable traffic, treading on shadow and slant broken light

my mother finds her way. By beer bottles, over smeared
Trojans, across leafmuck, she follows the track, clutching her
jacket close. The footbridge lofts her over the flashing cars
and sets her down, gently, among trees, where she is a child
in the weave of boughs, and leafshapes plait the breeze.

She fingers silver-green blades of the crack willow, she tests
                                                    dark grooves
of crack willow bark. The tree has a secret. Its branches pour
themselves back toward earth, and, my mother pauses, dredging
                                                    a breath
up out of her sluggish lungs. The blade leaves scratch
her fingertips, the corrugated bark

releases a privacy darker than cataract veils.
But slashed and ribboned, glimpsed through fronds,
the river hauls its cargo of argent light
and she advances, past basswood and crab apple clumps
along the tarmac where cyclists, joggers, rollerbladers

37

entranced in their varying orbits swoop
around her progress. With method, she reaches her bench,
she stations there. She sits columnular, fastened
to her difficult breath, and faces the river in late afternoon.
Behind her, voices. Before her, the current casts its glimmering

seine to a shore so distant no boundary scars
her retina, and only occasional sculls or sailboats flick
across her vision as quickened, condensing light.
There she sits, poised, while the fluent transitive Charles
draws off to the harbor and, farther, to the unseen sea

until evening settles, and takes her in its arms.

E. W.

Your purpled, parchment forearm
lodges an IV needle and valve;
your chest sprouts EKG wires;
your counts and pulses swarm

in tendrils over your head
on a gemmed screen: oxygen,
heart rate, lung power, temp
root you to the bed—

Magna Mater, querulous, frail,
turned numerological vine
whose every brilliant surge
convolutes the tale,

translates you to a life
shining beyond our own:
Come back to the world
we know the texture of—

demand your glasses back,
struggle into your clothes,
lean on me as you walk
into the summer dark

where you'll find once more your breath
and scold the wasted night.
Above us, satellites vastly wink.
Laugh. Come forth.

Diversion

Go, I say to myself, tired of my notebooks and my reluctant pen,
go water the newly transplanted sorrel and dill,
spriggy yet in their new humus and larger clay pots;
water artemisia, salvia, centaurea
which are classical, perennial, and have promised to spread
                                        their nimbus
of violet and silver through our patchy backyard
for summers to come, from poor soil.
Then I'll return indoors to the words copied
on the yellow legal pad,

her words
which I cannot shape;
which sentence me:

"There are things I prefer
   to forget—"
      (what things?) "Just,

things—" "Darling, I can't
   locate myself—" "Where
      are *you?*"

And if she, in her compassion, forgets
or doesn't know, I will perennially remember,
how I erase these messages
I later transcribe: one punch
of one button on the answering machine—

and how, with cruel
helpfulness
I have asked:

"Don't you remember?"

restoring to her a garden of incident
which she cannot keep, water, or tend,
and which will die, soon, from her ministrations.

Simile

As when her friend, the crack Austrian skier, in the story
she often told us, had to face
his first Olympic ski jump and, from
the starting ramp over the chute that plunged
so vertiginously its bottom lip
disappeared from view, gazed
on a horizon of Alps that swam and dandled around him
like toy boats in a bathtub, and he could not
for all his iron determination,
training and courage
ungrip his fingers from the railings of the starting gate, so that
his teammates had to join in prying
up, finger by finger, his hands
to free him, so

facing death, my
mother gripped the bedrails but still
stared straight ahead—and
who was it, finally,
who loosened
her hands?

From the Notebooks of Anne Verveine

I.

When his dogs leapt on Actaeon, he
cried (did he cry out?)—He flung

his arm to command, they tore his hand
from the wrist stump, tore

guts from his belly through the tunic, ripped
the cry from his throat.

That's how we know a god, when the facts
leap at the tenderest innards, and we know

the god is what we can't change. You
stood over me as I woke, I opened my eyes, I saw

that I'd seen and that it was too
late: the seeing

of you in the doorway with weak electric light
fanning behind you in the hall, and my room and narrow pallet
                                                    steeped in shadow

were what I couldn't change, and distantly
I wanted you, and, as distantly,

I heard the dogs, baying.

II.

And yet the fountain spends itself, and it is
in the clear

light of its losing that we seem
to take delight:

you dipped your hand in its running braid
to sprinkle my forehead, my lips.

Garden deities observed us: three nymphs
with moss staining their haunches, a pug-nosed faun.

The wound in water closed
perfectly around your gesture, erasing it,

so that only the glimmer, swiftly
drying, on my face recalled

our interruption
of the faultless, cold, passionate, perpetual

idea of the stream's descent—
which, unlike ours, would always be renewed.

III.

I kissed a flame, what did I expect.

Those days, you painted in fire. Tangerine, gold:
one would have had to be a pilgrim to walk
through that wall of molten glass.

And purification
could be conceived, if not
attained, only after many years,

in autumn, in a fire greater than yours,
though menstrual blood still tinged the threshold
and our ex-votos were sordid—scraps of blistered flesh

taped to kitsch prayer cards—and neither of us knew
the object of this exercise, except
having, inadvertently, each of us, burned

we recognized the smell
of wood smoke, the slow swirl
flakes of wood ash make in heavy air;

and we were ready, each in a private way, to make
the gifts the season required.
Mine was the scene

of my young self in your arms,
eyes in your eyes, clutched in the effort
to give each other away—when I glimpsed

behind your pleasure, fear; behind
fear, anger; and knew
in a bolt some gifts

conceal a greater gift.
I have kept it. Now I am ready to give it back
into darker flame

in this season of goldenrod, the ardent weed,
and Queen Anne's lace in its mantilla of ash.
And yet, how lumpishly, how stupidly I stand.

How much that is human will never burn.

IV.

And if you should answer?
I listened, years before I knew you, to the whine
of wind through the high stony pastures above my childhood
village;

I breathed lavender and thyme and burned my bare legs
on nettles, scraped them on thistles, and rubbed
the sore skin till it reddened all the more. When we

walked the uplands together, you burned your hand
and I kissed the crimsoning nettle-rash. "We are the Lords of
need,"
you said Hafiz said,

and I believed you, and we were.
In the rugs of your country, carmine is crushed
from insects, cochineal; saffron gold

46

is boiled from crocus starmens; and indigo
of heaven and fountain pools is soaked, hours upon hours,
from indigo leaves. "Like the angel Harut,"

you said, "We are in the calamity of love-desire."
The angel is chained by neck and knees, head down, in the pit
                                                    of Babel
for falling in love. Your carpets

told a different story: scarlet and saffron
blush as in Paradise, and God reveals himself
in wine, flame, tulips, and the light in a mortal eye.

All night you held me, sleepless, on my childhood cot in the
                                                    stone house;
all night the wind seethed through crags and twisted olive trees,
high on the scents of thyme and goat droppings. "All night,"

Hafiz sang, "I hope, the breeze of dawn will cherish the lovers."
But the breeze of dawn is the angel of death.
You are in your far landscape now, I am in mine:

the wind complains and I can't understand the words.
And if you should answer?
You, ten years away, in a different wind.

"We are in the calamity," Hafiz sang. "But tell the tale
of the minstrel and of wine, and leave time alone. Time
is a mystery no skill will solve." We should

thread words like pearls, you said, and the grateful sky
would scatter the Pleiades upon us
though we couldn't see, and that was long ago.

V.

The carpet is not a story. It is a place,
garden of crisscrossed pathways, labyrinth,
fountain, pool, and stream.

As though the fabric had ripped at the vanishing point
at the top of the street
of ashen façades and slate-sloped roofs, you stepped

through the gap, out of your own world.
I had already lost my world.
We met in a torn design

which we tore further, pulling the tall warp,
thread wrapped tightly around our fingers until it bit the flesh
and the rue de Lille unravelled.

I know about design: it's my job,
arranging other people's letters in star charts
that phosphoresce in the dark between the closed covers of
                                                                        books.

You knew about design from the holes
blown through your country.
We spoke in a language of no country on earth.

You moved slowly, in shadow, teaching the shadows
to echo my name. You ripped my shirt at the neck.
Was it The Beloved I held, holding you?

Down the middle of the carpet the river
weaves a thousand gray glimmers into the deeper green.
The river knows about mourning; that's its job.

How many years has it practiced? With such fleet fingers. A man woke me at dawn this morning, sobbing and cursing in the street, reeling from sidewalk to gutter and back again.

On my long gray street, the rue de Lille, where I still live.

Travel

43,000 feet below us
New England is a dun, scuffed, moulting carpet
with here and there a nick of light, as from broken glass.

Clouds trail across it like strands of grandmotherly hair.
With grave and steadfast shudders
we lunge through massive air.
We are flying south.

The inner Plexiglas windowpane,
chill to my fingertip, chill to my cheek,
has been incised by a human hand with zigzag and long cedilla.
The outer pane bears an ideograph of frost
resembling, now an intricate map of suburban roads and
                                                    driveways,
now a star.
            On the wing, the paint
blisters in gunmetal eczema.

Unbolted, my heart
is a missile
heading, in every sense, in the wrong direction.

Nightshade

Suddenly, looking once more at the Japanese elm, I saw
that you do not exist. No, not after years

of haunting, of your stepping just to the rim
of the snapshot, so that all I would see would be

a man's blurred silhouette half cropped, crowded to the edge
by the messy plates on the table, the loaded fruit bowl; not
                                                    after years

of your appearing suddenly in a farther room, the library
or den, in someone else's apartment, to beckon, then vanish;

not after your trick of standing under the drizzled street lamp
late at night so the fauve green light underscored your eye
                                                    sockets

and the slash of your jaw. I see now: you were Krishna, you were
Apollo, provisionally. Then they departed.

According to their nature. And the elm near the crown of
                                                    Peter's Hill
is left with out-flung branches— candelabra, octopus,

seaweed, lasso floating—-still trying to embrace
the orbed horizon which eludes but dallies in its boughs.

Where they cut the longest branch last summer, the stump
still gestures out toward the sky beyond the sky.

Walking home, l see lime-yellow berries of pokeweed
glossing into purple. The park's blood is up,

it makes its offering: knobbed crab apples, crimson
hawthorn berries with their crinkled parchment leaves,

and the little scarlet cornucopias of deadly nightshade,
and weeping larch, and each rose of Sharon with its
                                    hemorrhage at heart,

and jewelweed, and small tough marigolds. As evening floats
                                                    down,
the train-rumble and traffic-wheeze tighten their cincture

around the hill, where the Japanese elm fingers a vanishing
                                            arc of shade.
You are not waiting, lounging against the stone gate of the park;

you are not standing by the lindens along the street.
Two urchins greets me there, a boy and girl, clambering on the
                                                        trunk

of someone's parked car. "We're just sliding," they explain.
Now they rappel up a municipal letterbox. The little boy

is dark, the girl elfin, blonde, her nostrils and upper lip,
raw and brilliant from the feverish trickle of snot.

Antique

It doesn't happen these days, the retinal shock when
one of them slips by, shoots

a glance, is gone—We were singed but
kept breathing. They don't

appear after childhood. But
if he were to shiver into view, that

other one—lowercase kouros, lithe—
if he were to slide into sunlight here,

it would be on such a day: silver flakes
brisking in the woods as wind

whisks off mists and rainspatter, bark
ignites, birches sway: he can only step

from deepest shade. Do we have
darks enough to afford him

light? Over the pond, it's bronze, a Mycenaean
blade, black light smelted, that cleaves

sky from water, cirrus from leaf: he'd rise
froze the gash, the core

of arterial night. He knows
the weight and lightness of a sword, how one flesh falls

from another, and both are true as he stands
in his gleam of rain, godsweat, oil. We know it

differently. By clasping—which is all we know
how, in our heaviness, to do—clasping

subtraction, and hearing it cry aloud, nightly, in our arms.

Bonnard

It's like this: three large slices of
   world split into smaller, pulpy
      fistfuls of world within each

world-slice, and it all hurts, so
   debonair, so juicy: where
      is the woman, after all, the

center of this story? Well, we are
   mistaken. The center
      is a pillar of wrong

light, gone smooshed and overripe, re-
   flected, glassed, and we
      should be included but

we're not. It's not our house. The light
   doesn't smash us
      in the face or tilt

us backward out of our lives. Still,
   the column of garden
      hardly holds the story

together, and pomegranate seeds
   spill loose across the tiles and up
      the doorpost. So

many mirrors, you'd think, would give
   a point of view. They don't.
      They just ferment

sunlight into three species
　　of jam. The seeds
　　　of light will stick

in our teeth, the paste of light
　　wedge, unswallowed, in
　　　our throats. A flame

spurts in the toothy grate, but the soul
　　stays dark. She's bent, the
　　　soul, steeped in her confiture

of shadows; leans naked, bruised,
　　peripheral, half-
　　　erased. She's trying

to pray. She's trying to wash.
　　She's shivering in
　　　cold. She has understood

that never, in this life, will she be clean.

Piazza Pilo

The low stone and stucco wall opens
   in gaps; you can pass

through, cross diagonally, or meander
   within; you can sit on one of

eight slatted benches under elms and read the paper, you
   can sit on the wall and chat or

listen to the radio if it's night and you're young, you can walk
   your dog: the park accepts

all, its pebbles crunch under business shoes as under
   sneakers ambling, the dog-walker's

loiter, trudge of an elderly woman laden
   with plastic grocery bags, the full-tilt

charge of one boy chasing
   another. If you're crippled

or retarded you can sit here and the elms
   don't rush their friendliness, they are

just poking into frowzy leaf, it's April, they
   seem happy to have you, so are the

old German shepherd and her terrier friend, so are
   the grayish men with newspapers: you

can throne in your wheelchair and take the sun, or hunch
   on the wall and mumble. The park

knows how to receive, how to
   let go. Its puddles sink

(it rained last night) slowly out of
   sight. If you're sick, aging, in love,

the park shows you how nightingales pelt out songs
   at dawn where last night's trash

spills from the corner basket. You could
   let someone kiss you, slowly:

you could open your mouth to surprise, a
   gift the gods

grant with other gifts: the staggering heart,
   ashes on the tongue, long patience at slow

breakage. Prayer. The word
   "unhealed." The word "farewell."

Mistral II

I gave myself to the mistral, which had shouldered its way
down from the north, leaping the careful fields of France,
skimming the Alps, running the flat of its hand along the Rhône
to careen over this stretch of ultramarine and ancient sea
and seize the page out from under my pen.

The high eucalyptus shudder and surge,
the bamboo grove flashes its knives, yesterday's poem flies off:
we will all be changed in the quiet garden.
I have broken some forms, I am waiting to see
what survives this tumult of leaves
and cloudlight, what the sea will whip up from its jagged troughs
when spray shatters against the downward slicing veins of schist
and the hills bracing the valley wuther and groan.
The garden stays pegged to earth with its round metal tables
of pea-soup green, and its fan-patterns raked in tawny dirt,
and I stay pegged to the garden chair, but it was I who prayed
yesterday to make this refuge cry with a different breath,
hoping some new word would be snatched up out of my throat—
Its salt tang could be from sea wind, could be from tears.

Fear

I follow trying to pick up scraps of the poem as
you drop them you hide them but

they rustle I pry them out
from under cushions under the bed I pluck them like beaded
      curtain strings from

the whoosh of water in the shower where
you pretend to bathe when you are No One

No One is afraid of water No One
carves the soap so it won't touch his skin

it's the throb and splatter of water that
drums the color out of each day

good day hello hollow spider fingers sunken eyes antisoap for
      antimatter
you look out from a burned-out star

light-years away
still emitting

photons with that appealing deep affectionate dog's look of
      frightful understanding
a magic cloak of smell

No One will touch No One is safe No
One plays golf with interstellar swings so the ball never lands

TV keeps reciting the right spell day and night
the door is sealed shut with masking tape daylight strips human
       skin like acid

as long as the danger lived outside
me I couldn't write it

wants to crawl through the keyhole slide over the windowsill
it breathes in the shirts hanging in the closet

it rots the cheese
it lives in my breath it

hides in the pages of the poems of Paul Verlaine like a smear of
       shit
it has signed a contract in ink squeezed from stars

you are the gentlest prayer you
see where the shadow falls across each eye

of course of curse
song of all our days

you were empty so I drew a shrine
and it stayed empty

A Kosmos

You lay in your last sleep, not-sleep
head tilted stiffly to the right on the pillow
at a sharper angle than when you bent over poems,
year after year, and we plucked at each other's lines,

as if now you considered some even starker question.
Your IV tubes were gone. Your arms were bruised.
A blue cloth cap enfolded your pale, bald head.
It was too late to give you the lavender shawl I'd imagined

more for my sake than for yours.
Your mouth was suddenly tender, the mouth of a girl.
You had come very far, to come here.
Never one not to look at things squarely,

now you looked inward. Who knows what you saw.
And when, weeks later, we gathered
again at the house to say those formal farewells,
I went up to your study looking for *Leaves of Grass*

and found, instead, your orderly desk, unused,
your manuscripts neatly stacked, the framed
photographs of your girls, and, like a private message
from Whitman, who saw things whole, the small

dried body of a mouse. A kosmos, he too. He too, luckier.

After

The highway straight to the end of the world skims past
a ruined mall, Kmart with roof stove in,
acres of parking lots where weeds judder through cracks.

Police station smashed, but McDonald's still sells shocked grease.
In the concrete barracks nursing home all the old ones drowned
trapped in metal beds. A pink-flounced girl

floated for a week in sludge, legs apart, face down.
Write an inventory, make an index, stutter a psalm.
Raw sewage piped from trailers chokes the bayou

and I am thinking how to say "and" or whether "and"
is the word for the way, beyond the swamp, the ghosts of pines
and skeletal cypresses march for miles in haze

and how I lost count of slab after cement slab
where bungalows used to stand. Under the bridge
in a swarm of water hyacinths, alligators doze.

Draw a map of where X's brother hanged himself,
where Y died of diabetes when the drugs ran out,
and an invisible map of smoke patterns in the lungs

of the girl who hammers sheetrock and gessoes cracks.
Yesterday's eggs and oatmeal congeal on stacked plates,
the house rises from mouldy rubble and waist-high weeds.

At night, in the French Quarter, at the corner of Bourbon and
      Bienville,
two boys gargle love songs in the red light tide
sluicing from barroom windows into the street,

and as wind stoops to seize hard kisses from the current,
the tunes ride guitar riffs in updrafts over the roofs,
across the delirium tremens river toward the Gulf

where small waves lip the horizon, and sky stays mute.

Palaces

A city with a knife in its heart,
nerves exposed, arteries dangling, its temples to kingship,
religion, learning, and art
begrimed, and pock-marked by bullets,
or spruced, sand-blasted, and lacquered
to face the new market day. No wonder History
has a grim and elderly look.
She sits at the base of Schiller's statue,
manly, legs crossed, in her toga,
while her buxom sisters in negligé, Lyric,
Drama, and Philosophy, flirt with the passersby.
The boulevards convulse in excavations,
cranes rake the sky. The Palace of Tears
still runs with tears. In vacant lots
barrels protrude from puddles of khaki water,
pennants of shredded plastic shiver from chain-link fence.
Loss opens the way, I wrote in a letter
that was not a letter of love.
On Sophienstrasse, a small, grubby-faced boy
works with scholarly concentration
to dislodge a cobblestone the size of a scone
from the sidewalk in front of Queen Sophie Luisa's church.
The neighborhood shakes to the dentist's drill:
panel by coppery panel, girder by girder,
new labor dismantles old labor's Palast der Republik.

Forgiveness

The chestnut tree holds its votive candles aloft.
Blackbirds trill an invitation to evening, evening accepts.
The red fox skirts the terrace, and trots down to roll in the flower
       beds

which are mudded and empty. Small sailboats sidle
in their berths in the lakeside marina,
set free from ice: the water rustles in gray, silken moiré.

Spring is a breach birth,
umbilical cord at its neck, but twilight reaches
with capable hands to disengage it. Where you once stood

shouting; cursing, waving your arms,
a pool of silence gathers and the house exhales,
A house that no longer exists, a house in the mind.

And at this distance, do we know
which one of us cursed, who shouted?
Who waved indelible arms?

Forty-Second Street

The sidewalk gapes open down dark basement stairs `
You could fall there among kegs and cardboard cartons
spider-webs and planks   The brokers and the broken

pass on the street   Acacia leaves swirl up
in schools of golden flying fish   Then we see them
mashed in porridge in the gutter

In the back room of the library, old wooden card catalogues
tilt every which way, their tongues lolling out
An earthquake-stricken city emptied of ideas

as the wooden telephone booth in the marble hall
waits for phantoms
to ring with news of the other world

Outside, dropped boards clatter to the pavement
A truck clanks over a pothole, its hydraulic brake
squawks release   Cars shush by   Banks fail

East into morning Forty-Second Street
is a blinding, nickel-plated strip   Water hissed and gargled
all night in the bedroom wall

I made my prayer
to Nuestra Senora de la Soledad
and dropped *Shakti's Paperback Spiritual Guide to Self-Transformation*

in the trash with onion peels, melon rinds,
teabags, fishbones, and holiday photos
of impeccable children

Intermezzo, Piano Solo

Those teasing notes, descending, reverse themselves,
the whole piece mirrors itself upside and down.
Your fingers find their way, moving by heart
(sotto voce) from one thicket to another,
registering (dolente) in the soft tissue of fingerprints
what a poverty of notes, how richly strung—
as your kisses (perdendosi) repeat themselves
from one hour, one day, to the next, but never the same.
And now that you're gone (diminuendo), the andante strays
imperfectly in my mind. The nights are long,
meridional, raucous. I see now, purity
was just an effect of inexperience.
In the street below, the kids (crescendo) curse till dawn,
practice fellatio by streetlight, pressed to the wall.

From the Notebooks of Anne Verveine, VI

You are dead, therefore I write to you.
I am dead, therefore I write to you.
Did we ever kiss?The shadow airplane

swooped down to smack the tarmac silently.
That crash didn't crash. The kiss
did but dissipated

in air like phantom smoke
rising from my shadow chimney inching
its way all afternoon across

the neighbors' slanted roof—
heat gusts escaping up the flue and printing themselves
as visible ghosts trailing

off to a chilly Empyrean.
February gleams on the roof slates.
As if the fire were real. As if

the heart pumped real blood.

From the Notebooks of Anne Verveine, VII

Distance was the house in which I welcomed you.
But it was in the river
that we became cadence, there where the current braided

together again, after the stone bridge stanchion parted the stream.
It was to last only as long as the beauty lasted.
Do you believe in the soul?

Words torn from the void, wet and mewling.
Where we walked on the mountain, water
poured around us, surged up from springs, seethed

down in rivulets, rocky streams, and one long blinding cascade:
your kisses were an *eau-de-vie* and as bitter.
I am poured out like water.

Distance is feminine in French.
I held a knife to a man's throat and let him bleed quietly into a cup.
What does "us" mean?

Coiled serpentine headdress of Leonardo's woman:
you wanted her. I wanted you.
Chill sunlight flexing itself on the city river

gave me the emptiness I needed
to write these instructions: Sorrow
is a liqueur. Drink deep. We will all be consumed.

Earthworks

For Frederick Law Olmsted

I
Shadows

"The way of life is wonderful; it is by abandonment."
Emerson, "Circles"

Against icy morning light the sycamores
flex biceps, shrug shoulders, flaunt
broad arms, serpent-mottled   Hurrah they shout

or   Help   or   Pour down more sun
Disease bunches up in boles under the skin
and cranks the elbows   Malady we were taught

is picturesque   "Hollow trunk, dead arm, drooping bough"
wrote Mr. Gilpin, "splendid remnants of
decaying grandeur"   And other mischiefs

incident to trees   They fling their shadows
wide as archaic pitchforks, prong frozen soil
to dislodge five million ghostly cubic yards

of stone, earth, topsoil hauled to make
a park   The Park   The Central
Park   The central idea that all—

ward-heelers, dandies, urchins, freed slaves, desperadoes,
gents and ladies, the halt, the swift, the lame—
might come, might be drawn forth in courtesy, might

71

harmonize   Democracy is space
in which we flow   The shadows strike
back to the house in Hartford, curtains drawn

in daylight around the mother sunk in quilts,
no longer breathing in the laudanum gloom
and the small boy hardly breathing by the bed

Roots boil up in dragon coils from rock-hard earth
Elm, Norway maple, pin oak, honey locust, hickory
clutch and bunch secrets wrenched from below

where the mother lies in metamorphic dark
Bedrock mica schist at the core, littered above
with clay and gravel, gouged by glacier, shot

with granite dikes where magma probed and cooled
"No account kept of expenses from February 24 to March 12"
wrote Father the merchant   "Tuesday February 28

at one half past five p.m. my dear wife died"   And next
April—   "Married, $10.00"   The shadows press
child after child into the shale pages

of the Book of Earth   Charlotte measles, aged four   Owen
aged two   Ada aged six of bilious colic   "Her moans and cries
have been heartrending" writes young Fred

Anthologist of shadows   "The great principle of art,
breadth of light and shadow" counsels Sir Uvedale Price for whom
the eye should not be "stopt

and harassed by little disunited, discordant parts"
Nor is Democracy little discordant parts   Rhododendron,
azalea, rhodora, sweetgum, spice bush, green ash,

72

cucumber magnolia, Siberian elm   "The essence"
says Price   "is connection"   Olmsted and Vaux
loop tableland and meadow, hill, hollow, rock,

reservoir, lake and brook, East-West, North-South, above, below
in paths, roads, drives, and bridges cresting   Build
in solidest granite that the span

may loft across the death of brother John,
ghost-writer, confidante, comrade, closest soul
choked by tuberculosis far in southern France

"Dear, dear Fred   It appears we are not
to see one another any more   I am wild
with opium   I cannot comprehend

this suddenness—but I see it   I have no breath
Don't let Mary suffer while you are alive"
Price: "Twilight connects

what was before scattered; it fills up staring
meagre vacancies; it destroys
edginess; and by shadow as well as light to water

it increases its brilliance and softness"   Evening dissolves
opal and mother of pearl across the reservoir
Silences commissioners, bosses, office-seekers, first

citizens, journalists, bankers   Small waves lisp
and suck at the rim of blue ice
The wigeon tucks an emerald cheek under his wing

and drifts toward sleep as shade encumbers the elms

II
Slaughter

"Nothing is so fleeting as form; yet never does it quite deny itself."
Emerson, "History"

Where mud loosens from the clench of frost on raggedy slopes,
where willows blur in a fever of buds, where phoebes
skim to mud-clot nests on the joists of Bow Bridge

shanties yawed   Pig pens   Slaughterhouses   Bone-boiling sheds
Offal sank in the bog   Blood bubbled   "Hawkin led me through
vile sloughs in the black and unctuous slime—a practical man"

Olmsted, new to the Park works, to superintend
A literary man in city clothes to direct the gangs
A passion for drainage   "To the Board of Commissioners

of the Central Park   Gentlemen
To what extent shall the Park be drained?   By
what form of drains?   At what depth?

Thorough drainage a peculiar necessity for the site
Earthenware tubes four feet from the surface   I have
the honor to be your very

obedient servant"   To Asa Gray: "The site is rugged
Scarcely an acre of level or slope unbroken
by ledges   The board unmanageable, unqualified & liable

to permit any absurdity   Very faithfully yours"
Yet to hold John's widow Mary in his arms
is to hold a meadow of sweet young grass, to gather

74

dogwood petals soft as a horse's nose and press them to his cheek
is to kiss John awake and kiss him to sleep again
He tends John's children   (Charlie's eyes bad,

Charlotte broken out in boils)   Mary pregnant
and the servants all she-devils   Edward Kemp,
How to Lay Out a Garden: "What to avoid:

All kinds of Eccentricity, every sort of Sham,
Extreme Formality or Regularity of Plan . . .
What to attain: Simplicity, Connexion, Symmetry,

Variety in serpentine walks of different Curves,
and by Glades, Vistas, Recesses and Undulations
in the surface of the Ground . . . "   In the ruckus of sheets

he and Mary lie, simple, connected, recessed
in undulations and different curves   The baby kicks
within her and he rises to patrol the Park   "Dear Father

I have got the park into a capital discipline, a perfect
system like a machine, 1000 men at work
Health fair, only a lassitude & breaking down occasionally"

Typhoid   Fatigue   Over-taxed nervous energy
Is the marriage bed a meadow?   "Unity of effect"
Is the Park a battlefield?   The comptroller won't pay

to caulk new bridges, cuts off the pencil supply
His horse bolts, the phaeton smashes a post
Mary and the baby are flung   Olmsted cracks into a rock

His left thigh bone sticks through his trousers   Blood bubbles
Bone-boiling sheds   The scream of the hog   The baby dies
of cholera   Olmsted floats in fever   Where mud

75

loosens from the clench of frost, April 1861, Fort Sumter falls
Magnolia blossoms crushed in the muck in Central Park
"A great popular and democratic work" as the armies mass

Olmsted in Washington by the stinking canal
Abbatoir abutting the Monument   Pennsylvania Avenue a slough
Brandy   Tobacco juice   Recruits   Only ditches

for latrines "We knew then that we had to subjugate
slavery or be subjugated by it"
Frederick Law Olmsted   1861   Democracy

is space in which we flow   Democracy is large
disunited discordant parts   Democracy
spits and whistles   "The soldiers were dressed according

to individual caprice in caps with havelocks & straw hats
& red shirts, dirty, and slouched" writes Olmsted, secretary
of the Sanitary Commission   Scurvy   Malaria   Dysentery

Lincoln "in a cheap nasty French black cloth suit
just out of a carpet bag"   Clean up the camps
At Bull Run, glades, vistas, recesses and undulations

where green armies collide by a mustard-yellow stream
All day swaying in a *pas de deux*
Sluggish water where horses drown

Sun drains from meadows   Blood bubbles
Bone-boiling sheds   Where boys lie in coats too large
in sweet young grass   How soon flesh loosens

from the clench, of bone, and picnickers flee, their hampers crushed, their
bottles smashed   Horses scream   Unity of effect
Thigh bones stick out   Democracy takes

a very large design—

III
Trenches

"Beauty must come back to the useful arts." Emerson, "Art"

—a very large design, as chlorophyll
      pulses in the cells of live oak leaves
and the armies pinwheel through Virginia, up and down,

and summer 1862 is born in convulsions
      A ghost trails through Central Park in his army cap,
drooping mustache, gaunt cheeks, and flowing cape

who commandeered and stocked the hospital ships
      There he steps into the shade by the arc of a bridge
There he flickers a moment in a thicket of laurel

and dives into dense green   He shakes white blooms
      His phantom snail-track gleams on mud as if
the Chickahominy flowed here in Central Park

McClellan (that fine animal) drives his boys
      his hundred thousand recruits to capture Richmond
and squats them down in sludge and thunderstorms

77

and sleeps his malarial sleep at Seven Pines
      in an acoustic shadow   Scouts bungle   The generals miss
their cues   Bridges break   The surgeon general sends

no medicine, tents, supplies, while Olmsted works
      "with steady, feverish intensity till 4 a.m.,
sleeps on a sofa in his clothes and breakfasts on coffee

and pickles"   Hold the earthworks as the Confederates
      pour in   The picturesque, says Price, "various tints
of soil where the ground is broken by roots and tree trunks,

by tussocks of rushes, and by large stones
      partly whitened by air, partly covered by mosses"
As when corpses slowly sink into loam and that "want of form,

  that unshapen lumpish appearance" we cannot call
      beauty   Olmsted kneels on the deck, cradles
a dying man in his arms   Two hundred sick and mangled

on the *Daniel Webster* to New York   Eleven hundred
      on the *Ocean Queen* "He has the tact of a woman," writes
Miss Wormeley, "also much shrewdness and a quiet manner"

Scrub the ships   Haul the bodies by train down the peninsula
      to the docks   Bodies are earthworks   Hold them fast
In the boxcars the living, dying and dead lie packed in a jumble

Each man gulps another's last breath and broken groans
      and the rich slow reek of flesh-rot and dribbled feces
in the stacked dark   Thirty thousand dead in a week   Virginia gone

At Malvern Hill, "Not war, it was murder," wrote Confederate
      D. H. Hill   Mourning doves
burble requiems in the high, silvery beeches in Central Park

and the elms, as Gilpin foretold, receive grand masses of light
        So much labor to hold the soul
in one small, earthenware vessel, one body easily smashed

with someone's rigid and filthy heel in its mouth, another's
        fist in its eye   Earthworks and trenches
collapse as Fred's apprentice irrigation ditch years back

on the Onondoga Farm gullied out in rain
        and flooded the garden   Each night he read
Upham's *Principles of the Interior or Hidden Life*

Now Mary guards the new baby, fistful of delicate clay,
        Marion, squinch-faced in a bundle of blankets, while Olmsted,
tracks 1863 to Vicksburg on trains and boats, "floors shiny

with tobacco juice and apple cores," "palatial hotels," "the dreariest
        American humbug"   At Murfreesboro the fields
charred, trees twisted and blackened, dead horses rot

From Cairo to Memphis down river, the Belle
        huffs through desolation   Grant's camp above Vicksburg
Two long lines of graves on the levee where vultures waft

 over roses and yellow jasmine, and mocking birds trill
        "The effect of slavery," wrote Olmstead, "is universally
ruinous"   On cross currents, sunbeams knife

the eyeball in shifting glare   Grant is "small,
        quiet, gentle, modest, with quick common sense" and he gives
a steamer to carry the wounded   July 4

Vicksburg surrenders, and Gettysburg ends in a gasp and rictus
        We made a shape and we called it a country
We didn't know how much blood it would take to fill the idea

or whose, by lash or by sword   Or by what
     crossed pathways, maps lost and hardly remembered
or that earthworks, to stand, demand stone and a mortar of blood

The Park gathers us into July's juicy, sauntering dream,
     bare-shouldered frolic and shady deals down curving paths,
holding hands, pushing strollers, in the sweet tickle of sweat

as the high, massed foliage shudders and shuffles its darks
     It hushes its blights   A pale blue balloon
quavers in an updraft, curtseys, and swoons off, invisible, free—

IV

Hollows

" . . . the same condition of an infinite remoteness . . ." Emerson,
"Friendship"

—Free to draw his own conclusions, and to stroll
among hawthorn, persimmon and spindle-trees in the Ramble

he designed in order to

lose himself, so that others might lose
themselves, might be "weaned from debasing

pursuits and brutalizing

pleasures," he meanders, off-hours   Free
for a spell from drafting table, memoranda and orders for new parks,

free from his father's

80

gentle dying, from Tammany commissioners and *The Spoils of the Park*,
he kicks through folios of fallen leaves and their

whispered obituaries

Where the path dips, it might be Avernus   That hulking shade,
Lincoln, whose "frankness and courageous

directness" he'd finally

seen   That tremor by the ash tree, that rustle in the underbrush, Owen,
his son, dead at twenty-four   A chill in the air   An iron taste

An early dusk as boughs

strip down   Pages flutter to earth, his thousands of joyless,
laborious sheets, "lines spaced far apart for his interlinear

corrections, and corrections

of corrections until the spaces between the lines, the margins, and even the
      back
of the page are crowded with his crabbed and hasty script"   Neuralgia

Insomnia   His "impracticable

temper and irritable brain" never followed straight lines   The clubs—
Century, Union League, Saturday Club—, *The Nation* editorial board,

sift into compost

The granite ledge presses moist into his palm   Spine of the Park   A rock
with its own constitution, its own amendments, it lends itself

81

only partly to his

designs   His work "everywhere arrested, wrenched, mangled and misused—
a mortification"   Branches lopped   Roads rammed through

meadows, and "that excessive

materialism of purpose in which we are, as a people, so cursedly
absorbed," absorbs park after park   Brooklyn   Boston   Buffalo   He stands
     in shade,

the sociable man beyond

society, where the brain puckers in gulches and hollows, and solitude
is perfected   He made a shape for the errant soul,

the hidden life, the

refugee   A reverie beyond
the touch of wife, son, nephew, fame, doctors or the firm's future, beyond
     the gaze

of the painter who sees

him as white-bearded, benevolent sage of Capitalist rhododendrons
Dementia has its own genius

He essays a path

into the rock's deep crevice and disappears   He barely disturbs
the litter of leaves   We would not know him, but as our season

darkens, we still walk

in the privacy he traced for us, and the sycamores
ravel a canopy of cloud with knowing fingers over our heads

Liszt, Overheard

Jet-lagged, half-insomniac, I lie in a dim tower
in a foreign college as piano notes ripple up
the winding stair. It's medieval here,
spliced Renaissance spliced late Victorian.
I'm an emigrant from my life. Now a violin
teases the piano, a cello breathes heavily on both—
an audience must be straining forward in a panelled hall.
How many years have I half-heard
a music meant for others? The chestnut trees
shrug epaulets and fringes in the night wind.
Black tulips sway. An arpeggio falls downstairs.
Your face surges, known and strange, its history drawn
by an Old Master who worked only in the dark.

Aubade

Silver gelatin the fine outline of the window sash at dawn
but morning turned blind eyes to us nor could
I see you   Sleep had cobwebbed you like a pharaoh
and later when we walked in the frozen field we cracked every mirror
Swamp grasses ticked against each other
Metallic puddles showed us nothing not even our shadows
My shadow asked your shadow where was the lost child
Mahler said for a soft sound don't give it to the oboe but
only to some monster instrument that must struggle and force
beyond its natural range to murmur or hum
We outpaced our shadows   We were looking for the place
where light would cry out when ice sliced its hands
but we found instead the crimson reishi fungus ruffled in its
       petticoat
Ganoderma lucidum from which a healing tea could be boiled
though we abstained left it on its stump and returned with our palms empty
hungry for night eager
for another dawn

Ghost in a Red Hat

—these cabbages under full sail, these ancient walls
        smothered in ivy and wisteria with its purple froth:

in my middle age and sensible girth

I remember

starving.
I didn't know why.

I practiced being a ghost.
        I was a girl, I thought

this was how one became
        a woman. I lived in a village
        in Italy, it was picturesque, I was not

picturesque. That was the project:
I gnawed stale bread, roamed vineyards and olive groves,
drew portraits of artichoke plants under twisted trees,
        recited Petrarch and grew

        so thin I was a dazzling
        knifeblade in my new white pants.

The old grandmother quietly cursed in a corner.
Her family ignored her. They ignored me.
I recited more Petrarch and bought a broad-brimmed crimson straw hat.

        What to do with this girl?

She learned to survive long spells of dryness.
She embraced strangers and they stayed strange.
She painted still lifes and they stayed still.
She dreamed she attended a soirée at a Soho loft
      Where the main dish on a platter garnished with parsley
      Was a woman's naked torso, roasted, belly down, crisply hot.

She looked for the small flame guttering in a sacred jar.

Giving birth was one way. Holding a dying man's hand was another.
She buried small animals, with appropriate rites, in the back yard.

    And here are the generations: water and fire

      begat turpentine which joined
      earth and brought forth

          color from mineral loins and boiled-down vegetable soul.

      So steeped and soaked, this land where I live now,
          so rushing in rain,
roof tiles bristle in moss, close-woven or feathery, sprigging with spores—

The cemetery teems: lichen, honeysuckle, roses.
      Little mildewed photographs under glass.
Enemies make peace.
          Centuries fall through limestone cracks.

And Edith came up the street this morning
      to bring me *Le Monde* and *La Revue des deux mondes*

      and a packet of fresh goat cheese

before setting out, in rain, on her drive to the Dordogne.

NOTES

"To Max Jacob" and "Max Jacob at St-Benoît"

Max Jacob (1876–1944) was a French Jewish poet and painter, close companion in the early days of Cubism to Picasso, Apollinaire, and Derain. He converted to Roman Catholicism in 1915 (with Picasso as his improbable godfather), and spent his last years in close connection to the Benedictine monastery of St. Benoît-sur-Loire. He was arrested by the Nazis in 1944, and died of pneumonia in the concentration camp of Drancy outside of Paris. He was lucky; his name was on the list for the next transport to Auschwitz.

"Departure"

The title comes from Max Beckmann's triptych in the Museum of Modern Art in New York. The poem splices quotations from the Italian poet Guido Guinizelli (1240?–1274) and from Beckmann (1884–1950). I have translated from Guinizelli's "Al cor gentil rempaira sempre Amore"; the lines from Beckmann are adapted from remarks recorded in *Max Beckmnann's Triptychs* by Charles S. Kessler (Cambridge: Harvard University Press, 1970).

"Mud" smashes up and incorporates lines from Wilfred Owen and David Jones, as John Walker does in his great sequence of paintings inspired by World War I.

"From the Notebooks of Anne Verveine"

Anne Verveine is an imaginary French poet. She was born in 1965 in the village of Magagnosc in the Alpes Maritimes, and attended the *lycée* in Grasse. She never studied in a university. She lived obscurely in Paris, avoiding literary society and working as a typographer and designer for a small publisher of art books. She published a few poems in provincial journals, but no book of her own work. She was last seen hitchhiking in Uzbekistan in August 2000; is presumed kidnapped or dead. Her sister found these poems in notebooks in the poet's small apartment in Paris after her disappearance. I translate them.

"A Kosmos" is an elegy for the poet and nonfiction writer Deborah Tall.

"Earthworks"

"Earthworks": the poem commemorates Frederick Law Olmsted, who designed Central Park in New York City with Calvert Vaux. Olmsted was also the first Executive Secretary of the Sanitary Commission, the civilian organization founded to succor and retrieve the wounded from the battlefields of the Civil War. The Commission later became the Red Cross. I have drawn on many works for this poem. Among Olmsted's writings, I read *Walks and Talks of an American Farmer in England* (1852); *Journeys and Explorations in the Cotton Kingdom* (1861); *The Cotton Kingdom: A Traveller's Observations on Cotton and Slavery in the American Slave States. Based Upon Three Former Volumes of Journeys and Investigations* (1862); *Slavery and the South 1852–1857* in *The Papers of Frederick Law Olmsted*, vol. II, edited by Charles Capen McLaughlin and Charles. E. Beveridge (1981); the correspondence and reports concerned with the design of Central Park in *Creating Central Park 1857–1861* in *The Papers of Frederic Law Olmsted*, vol. III (McLaughlin and Beveridge, 1983); and *The Spoils of the Park* (1881). I also quote from the books Olmsted loved and kept near him: Edward Kemp's *How to Lay Out a Garden* (2nd ed., 1858); Ruskin's *Modern Painters* (1843); Sir Uvedale Price's *On the Picturesque* (1794); William Gilpin's *Forest Scenery* (1791), Andrew Jackson Downing's *The Fruits and Fruit Trees of America* (1850); and Emerson's *Essays: First Series* (1841). The drawings in *The Central Park: Original Drawings* (1980) were extremely useful. Laura Wood Roper's biography, *FLO: A Biography of Frederick Law Olmsted* (1973), provided the foundation. A year at the Cullman

Center at the New York Public Library offered the time, peace of mind, and access to books that made the poem possible.

"...the painter who sees
him as white-bearded, benevolent sage of Capitalist rhododendrons":
John Singer Sargent painted Olmsted's portrait in 1895 at Biltmore in Asheville, North Carolina, the estate of George Washington Vanderbilt II. The design of the grounds of Biltmore was Olmsted's last major project.

ACKNOWLEDGMENTS

These poems are from collections published by W. W. Norton, and are reprinted with grateful acknowledgment.

"The Cormorant" appeared in *The Best American Poetry* 1990, edited by Jorie Graham and David Lehman. "Hagar" was printed in *American Religious Poems*, edited by Harold Bloom and Jesse Zuba, Library of America, 2006. "Song" appeared in *The Best American Poetry 1991*, edited by Mark Strand and David Lehman. "Necrophiliac" appeared in *The Best American Poetry 1992*, edited by Charles Simic and David Lehman, and in *The Best of the Best American Poetry 2013* edited by Robert Pinsky and David Lehman. "Bonnard" appeared in *Words for Images: A Gallery of Poems*, edited by John Hollander and Joanna Weber, Yale University Art Gallery, 2001. "Departure" was reprinted in *The Best American Poetry 1998*, edited by John Hollander and David Lehman; "Diversion" in *The Best American Poetry 1997*, edited by James Tate and David Lehman, and in *The Best of the Best American Poetry 1988–1997*, edited by Harold Bloom and David Lehman. "From the Notebooks of Anne Verveine, VI" was published in *The Imaginary Poets*, edited by Alan Michael Parker. "From the Notebooks of Anne Verveine, VI and VII" were published in French translation by Aude Pivin in the journal *Pleine Marge* in France. The following poems appeared in *Joining Music with Reason: 34 Poets, British and American, Oxford 2004–2009*, edited by Christopher Ricks: "A Kosmos," "Aubade," "Intermezzo, Piano Solo," "Liszt, Overheard."

www.ingramcontent.com/pod-product-compliance
Lightning Source LLC
Chambersburg PA
CBHW050349110426
42812CB00008B/2411